FAVORITE BRAND
NAME RECIPES™

American Heart
Association®

Learn and Live SM

Recipes
for
the Heart

Go Red™
for women

Publications International Ltd.

Favorite Brand Name Recipes at www.fbnr.com

Front cover: Stuffed Spinach Rolls *(page 38)*
Back cover: *(counterclockwise from top):* Oven-Puffed Pancakes (Dutch
Baby) *(page 56),* Chilled Strawberry-Raspberry Soup *(page 10),*
Cheese-Smothered Chicken with Quick Salsa *(page 22)*

ISBN: 1-4127-2198-9

Manufactured in U.S.A.

8 7 6 5 4 3 2 1

contents

The American Heart Association's Go Red For
Women campaign is spreading the word about
women and heart disease

Cardiovascular disease is the No. 1 cause of death for women
in America, so learn what you can do to reduce your risk

Sign up today for free programs that
will help you improve your heart health

Programs and information to help you
join the fight against cardiovascular
disease

Real-life stories from five courageous
women who have dealt with heart
attack or stroke

recipes

The American Heart Association dietary guidelines help you make sensible choices about the foods you eat. By following these guidelines—which apply to all healthy people over the age of two—you will enjoy the best of nature's bounty, and you may reduce your risk for heart disease and stroke.

Six Simple Steps to Good Nutrition

1. Enjoy a wide variety of foods from each food group.

♥ Six or more servings of grain and whole-grain products and legumes each day. *For example...*
  - *1 slice bread*
  - *1 cup flaked cereal*
  - *½ cup cooked cereal or pasta*

♥ Five or more servings of vegetables and fruits each day. *For example...*
  - *1 medium piece fruit*
  - *1 cup leafy greens*
  - *¾ cup fruit or vegetable juice*
  - *½ cup cooked vegetables*

♥ Three or more servings of fat-free or low-fat milk products for most adults. *For example...*
  - *1 cup milk or yogurt*
  - *½ cup cottage cheese*
  - *1 ounce cheese*

♥ Two servings of lean meat, poultry, seafood, or vegetarian protein each day. Include at least two servings of fish each week, preferably fatty fish. *For example...*
  - *3 ounces cooked meat, poultry, or seafood*
  - *½ cup cooked beans or lentils*
  - *¼ cup canned tuna or salmon*

2. Choose a diet low in saturated and trans fats. Replace these fats with the healthful polyunsaturated and monounsaturated fats.

3. Balance your food intake with physical activity to achieve and maintain a healthy weight.

4. Limit your daily intake of dietary cholesterol to less than 300 milligrams.

5. Keep your intake of sodium to less than 2,400 milligrams per day. (If you have had a heart attack or have coronary heart disease, your doctor may recommend lower limits.)

6. If you drink alcohol, limit yourself to one drink per day if you're a woman and two drinks per day if you're a man. If you don't drink, don't start.

How the Recipes Are Analyzed

- Each analysis is for a single serving; garnishes or optional ingredients are not included.
- When ingredient options are listed, the first one is analyzed.
- Values for saturated, monounsaturated, and polyunsaturated fats are rounded and may not add up to the amount listed for total fat. Total fat also includes other fatty substances and glycerol.
- The reduced-fat cheese we use for analysis has no more than 6 grams of fat per ounce.
- When meat, poultry, or seafood is marinated and the marinade is discarded, we calculate only the amount of marinade absorbed.
- Meat statistics are based on cooked lean meat with all visible fat removed.
- We use the abbreviations "g" for gram and "mg" for milligram.

starters

Cherry Tomatoes with Kalamata Cream Cheese

Serves 6; 2 cherry tomatoes and ½ tablespoon cream cheese mixture per serving

Kalamata Cream Cheese

- **3** tablespoons light garden vegetable or herb cream cheese spread
- **6** kalamata olives, finely chopped
- **2** tablespoons finely snipped fresh parsley
- **¼** teaspoon dried basil, crumbled

- **12** cherry tomatoes

In a small bowl, stir together kalamata cream cheese ingredients using a rubber scraper.

Cut a very thin slice from top of each tomato. Place tomatoes with cut side down on paper towels to blot.

Place about ¾ teaspoon cream cheese mixture on cut side of each tomato. Arrange tomatoes on a serving plate.

DIETARY EXCHANGES ½ Fat

NUTRIENTS PER SERVING Calories 31; Total Fat 2 g; Saturated Fat 1 g; Polyunsaturated Fat 0 g; Monounsaturated Fat 1 g; Carbohydrates 2 g; Sugar 0 g; Fiber 1 g; Cholesterol 5 mg; Protein 1 g; Sodium 95 mg

Chilled Strawberry-Raspberry Soup

Serves 5; 1 cup per serving

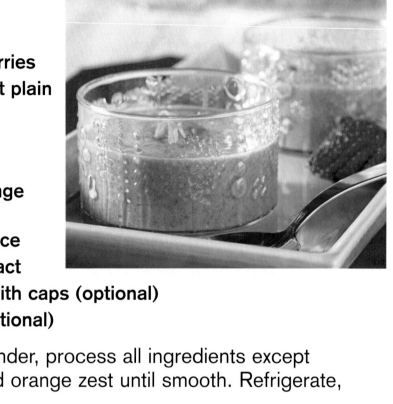

- 2 cups whole fresh strawberries
- 1 cup fresh or frozen unsweetened raspberries
- 1 cup fat-free or low-fat plain yogurt
- 2 tablespoons sugar
- 2 tablespoons honey
- ½ teaspoon grated orange zest
- 1¾ cups fresh orange juice
- ½ teaspoon vanilla extract
- 5 whole strawberries with caps (optional)
- 5 orange zest curls (optional)

In a food processor or blender, process all ingredients except strawberries with caps and orange zest until smooth. Refrigerate, covered, to chill if desired.

Make strawberry fans for garnish by thinly slicing each strawberry lengthwise to, but not all the way through, the cap. Press down gently on cap end to separate slices into a fan.

To serve, ladle soup into bowls. Place a curl of orange zest on top and a strawberry fan beside each serving.

DIETARY EXCHANGES 1 Fruit, 1 Other Carbohydrate, ½ Skim Milk

NUTRIENTS PER SERVING Calories 142; Total Fat 0.5 g; Saturated Fat 0 g; Polyunsaturated Fat 0 g; Monounsaturated Fat 0 g; Carbohydrates 32 g; Sugar 28 g; Fiber 3 g; Cholesterol 1 mg; Protein 4 g; Sodium 40 mg

Avocado and White Bean Dip

Serves 8; 2 tablespoons per serving

- ½ **15-ounce can no-salt-added navy beans, rinsed and drained**
- ½ **medium avocado, peeled and seeded**
- ¼ **cup fat-free or low-fat plain yogurt**
- 2 **tablespoons fat-free milk**
- 1 **tablespoon fresh lime juice**
- 1 **medium garlic clove**
- ½ **teaspoon ground cumin**
- ¼ **teaspoon salt**
- ⅛ **teaspoon cayenne**

In a food processor or blender, process all ingredients until smooth, scraping bowl frequently.

DIETARY EXCHANGES ½ Starch, ½ Fat

NUTRIENTS PER SERVING Calories 50; Total Fat 2 g; Saturated Fat 1 g; Polyunsaturated Fat 0.5 g; Monounsaturated Fat 1 g; Carbohydrates 6 g; Sugar 2 g; Fiber 2 g; Cholesterol 0 mg; Protein 2 g; Sodium 83 mg

Cook's Tip

You can make this dip up to 24 hours in advance. Cover and refrigerate until ready to serve. The acid in the lime keeps the avocado from turning dark.

Baked-Pear and Goat Cheese Salad

Serves 4; 1½ cups salad greens, 2 tablespoons dressing, and 1 stuffed pear half per serving

- 1½ tablespoons walnuts, finely chopped
- ½ ounce soft goat cheese
- 2 pears (about 8 ounces each), peeled, halved, and cored
  Vegetable oil spray
- ¼ cup raspberry vinegar
- ¼ cup honey
- ¼ teaspoon ground ginger
- ¼ teaspoon ground cinnamon
- ¼ teaspoon salt
- ⅛ teaspoon crushed red pepper flakes
- 6 cups mixed salad greens (spring mix preferred)

Preheat oven to 400°F.

Heat a small skillet over medium-high heat. Dry-roast walnuts for 1 to 2 minutes, or until beginning to brown, stirring constantly. Pour into a small bowl.

Stir goat cheese into walnuts.

Place pears on a baking sheet. Spoon walnut mixture into center of each pear. Lightly spray pears with vegetable oil spray.

Bake for 20 minutes, or until pears are just tender.

Meanwhile, in a small bowl, stir together remaining ingredients except salad greens.

To serve, arrange salad greens on plates. Spoon dressing over salad greens. Place a warm pear half on each serving.

DIETARY EXCHANGES 1 Fruit, 1 Other Carbohydrate, ½ Fat

NUTRIENTS PER SERVING Calories 156; Total Fat 3 g; Saturated Fat 0.5 g; Polyunsaturated Fat 1.5 g; Monounsaturated Fat 0.5 g; Carbohydrates 33 g; Sugar 26 g; Fiber 4 g; Cholesterol 2 mg; Protein 3 g; Sodium 180 mg

main
dishes

Sirloin Steak with Sweet and Tangy Orange Sauce

Serves 4; 3 ounces beef per serving

- ¼ cup plus 2 tablespoons steak sauce
- 2 tablespoons sugar
- 2 teaspoons grated orange zest
- ¼ teaspoon salt
- ⅛ teaspoon crushed red pepper flakes
  Vegetable oil spray
- 1 pound boneless top sirloin steak (about ¾ inch thick), all visible fat discarded

In a small bowl, stir together steak sauce, sugar, orange zest, salt, and red pepper flakes.

Lightly spray a broiler rack and pan with vegetable oil spray. Put steak on rack. Spoon 2 tablespoons sauce over steak. Let stand for 15 minutes.

Preheat broiler.

Broil about 4 inches from heat for 3 minutes. Turn over. Spread remaining sauce over steak. Broil for 6 minutes, or until desired doneness. Remove from broiler and let stand on a cutting board for 5 minutes before thinly slicing.

DIETARY EXCHANGES ½ Other Carbohydrate, 3 Lean Meat

NUTRIENTS PER SERVING Calories 201; Total Fat 6.5 g; Saturated Fat 2.5 g; Polyunsaturated Fat 0 g; Monounsaturated Fat 2.5 g; Carbohydrates 10 g; Sugar 6 g; Fiber 1 g; Cholesterol 67 mg; Protein 25 g; Sodium 553 mg

Weeknight Beef Skillet Casserole

Serves 4; 1½ cups per serving

Vegetable oil spray
12 ounces lean ground beef
1 medium green bell pepper, finely chopped
10 ounces frozen mixed vegetables
1 8-ounce can no-salt-added tomato sauce
1 tablespoon low-sodium Worcestershire sauce
½ tablespoon dried Italian seasoning, crumbled
2 teaspoons sugar
6 ounces dried no-yolk egg noodles
¼ cup snipped fresh parsley
¾ teaspoon salt

Heat a 12-inch nonstick skillet over medium-high heat. Remove from heat and lightly spray with vegetable oil spray (being careful not to spray near a gas flame). Cook beef for 3 minutes, or until browned, stirring frequently. Pour into a colander and rinse under hot water to remove excess fat. Drain well. Wipe skillet with paper towels. Return beef to skillet.

Stir in bell pepper. Cook for 3 minutes, or until just tender-crisp, stirring frequently.

Stir in mixed vegetables, tomato sauce, Worcestershire sauce, Italian seasoning, and sugar. Bring to a boil over medium-high heat. Reduce heat and simmer, covered, for 20 minutes, or until green beans (in mixed vegetables) are tender.

Meanwhile, prepare noodles using package directions, omitting salt and oil. Drain well, reserving ¾ cup cooking water. Stir noodles, reserved water, parsley, and salt into beef mixture.

DIETARY EXCHANGES 3 Starch, 1 Vegetable, 3 Very Lean Meat

NUTRIENTS PER SERVING Calories 332; Total Fat 3.5 g; Saturated Fat 1 g; Polyunsaturated Fat 0.5 g; Monounsaturated Fat 1.5 g; Carbohydrates 50 g; Sugar 10 g; Fiber 5 g; Cholesterol 38 mg; Protein 23 g; Sodium 533 mg

Throw and Go Chili

Serves 4; about 1¼ cups per serving

   Vegetable oil spray
12 ounces lean ground beef
 1 16-ounce can no-salt-added dark red kidney beans, rinsed and drained
 1 14.5-ounce can diced tomatoes with onions, celery, and bell peppers
12 ounces frozen bell pepper stir-fry mix (bell peppers and onions)
 1 tablespoon chili powder
 ½ tablespoon instant coffee granules
 1 teaspoon ground cumin
 ½ teaspoon sugar
 ¼ teaspoon salt
 ¼ cup fat-free or light sour cream (optional)

Heat a 12-inch skillet over medium-high heat. Remove from heat and lightly spray with vegetable oil spray (being careful not to spray near a gas flame). Cook beef for 3 minutes, or until browned, stirring frequently. Pour into a colander and rinse under hot water to remove excess fat. Drain well. Wipe skillet with paper towels. Return beef to skillet. Increase heat to high.

Stir in beans, tomatoes, bell peppers, chili powder, coffee granules, cumin, and sugar. Bring to a boil over medium-high heat. Reduce heat and simmer, covered, for 30 minutes.

Stir in salt. Let stand for 10 minutes to absorb flavors.

To serve, ladle chili into bowls. Top each serving with a dollop of sour cream.

DIETARY EXCHANGES 1 Starch, 3 Vegetable, 3 Very Lean Meat

NUTRIENTS PER SERVING Calories 259; Total Fat 3.5 g; Saturated Fat 1 g; Polyunsaturated Fat 0.5 g; Monounsaturated Fat 1.5 g; Carbohydrates 32 g; Sugar 11 g; Fiber 7 g; Cholesterol 38 mg; Protein 24 g; Sodium 601 mg

Herbed Pork Tenderloin

Serves 4; 3 ounces pork per serving

- 1 **pound pork tenderloin, all visible fat and silver skin discarded**
- ¼ **cup fat-free or light Italian salad dressing**
- 2 **teaspoons dried oregano, crumbled**
- 1 **teaspoon grated lemon zest**
  Vegetable oil spray
- ¼ **teaspoon dried rosemary, crushed, or dried tarragon, crumbled**
- ¼ **teaspoon pepper**
- ¼ **teaspoon paprika**

In a large resealable plastic bag, combine pork, salad dressing, oregano, and lemon zest. Seal bag. Turn bag to coat pork completely. Refrigerate for 8 to 12 hours, turning occasionally.

Preheat oven to 425°F. Line a baking sheet with aluminum foil. Lightly spray foil with vegetable oil spray.

Remove pork from marinade. Most of marinade will adhere to pork; don't scrape it off. Discard any marinade still in bag. Put pork on baking sheet. Sprinkle pork with rosemary, pepper, and paprika. Tuck thinner end of pork under for even cooking.

Bake for 24 minutes, or until internal temperature of pork measures 155°F and it is barely pink in center. Let stand for 5 minutes before slicing.

DIETARY EXCHANGES ½ Other Carbohydrate, 3 Lean Meat

NUTRIENTS PER SERVING Calories 157; Total Fat 4 g; Saturated Fat 1.5 g; Polyunsaturated Fat 0.5 g; Monounsaturated Fat 1.5 g; Carbohydrates 5 g; Sugar 2 g; Fiber 0 g; Cholesterol 74 mg; Protein 24 g; Sodium 197 mg

Layers of Flavors Mexican Salad

Serves 4; 2 cups per serving

- 5 cups shredded romaine
- ½ cup fat-free or light ranch dressing
- 1 tablespoon fresh lime juice
- ¾ teaspoon ground cumin
- ⅛ teaspoon red hot-pepper sauce
- 8 ounces grape tomatoes or cherry tomatoes, halved (about 1½ cups)
- ½ 15-ounce can no-salt-added black beans, rinsed and drained
- ½ 4-ounce can chopped mild green chiles, rinsed and drained
- 2 tablespoons snipped fresh cilantro
- 1 cup shredded fat-free sharp Cheddar cheese

Spread romaine in a 13×9×2-inch baking dish.

In a small bowl, stir together dressing, lime juice, cumin, and hot-pepper sauce. Spoon over romaine.

In order listed, add one layer of each of remaining ingredients.

DIETARY EXCHANGES ½ Starch, 1 Vegetable, 1 Other Carbohydrate, 1½ Very Lean Meat

NUTRIENTS PER SERVING Calories 162; Total Fat 0.5 g; Saturated Fat 0 g; Polyunsaturated Fat 0 g; Monounsaturated Fat 0 g; Carbohydrates 27 g; Sugar 6 g; Fiber 5 g; Cholesterol 5 mg; Protein 14 g; Sodium 590 mg

Cheese-Smothered Chicken with Quick Salsa

Serves 4; 1 chicken breast half and ¼ cup salsa per serving

Vegetable oil spray

4 **boneless, skinless chicken breast halves (about 4 ounces each), all visible fat discarded**

½ **teaspoon ground cumin**

1 **4-ounce can chopped mild or hot green chiles, rinsed and drained if desired**

½ **cup fat-free or part-skim shredded mozzarella cheese**

Quick Salsa

1 **cup diced tomatoes**

2 **tablespoons snipped fresh cilantro**

¼ **teaspoon grated lime zest**

1 **tablespoon lime juice**

¼ **teaspoon salt**

Preheat oven to 400°F. Lightly spray a nonstick baking sheet with vegetable oil spray.

Place chicken in a single layer on baking sheet. Top each piece with cumin, then chiles, then mozzarella.

Bake for 20 minutes, or until no longer pink in center. Transfer to plates.

Meanwhile, in a small bowl, stir together salsa ingredients.

To serve, spoon salsa over chicken.

DIETARY EXCHANGES 1 Vegetable, 1 Very Lean Meat

NUTRIENTS PER SERVING Calories 164; Total Fat 1.5 g; Saturated Fat 0.5 g; Polyunsaturated Fat 0.5 g; Monounsaturated Fat 0.5 g; Carbohydrates 5 g; Sugar 1 g; Fiber 2 g; Cholesterol 68 mg; Protein 31 g; Sodium 489 mg

Hoisin Chicken and Snow Peas

Serves 4; 3 ounces chicken, ½ cup vegetable mixture, and ½ cup rice per serving

- 1¼ **cups water**
- 1 **cup uncooked quick-cooking brown rice**
- 2 **teaspoons grated peeled gingerroot**
- ½ **teaspoon ground turmeric (optional)**
- ¼ **cup all-fruit apricot spread**
- 3 **tablespoons hoisin sauce**
- 1 **tablespoon cider vinegar**
- ⅛ **teaspoon crushed red pepper flakes (optional)**
  Vegetable oil spray
- 1 **pound boneless, skinless chicken breasts, all visible fat discarded, cut into 2×¼-inch strips**
- 2 **teaspoons canola oil**
- 2 **medium onions, cut lengthwise into thin strips**
- 6 **ounces snow peas, trimmed if fresh, thawed if frozen**
- ¼ **teaspoon salt**

In a medium saucepan, bring water to a boil. Stir in rice, gingerroot, and turmeric. Reduce heat and simmer, covered, for 10 minutes, or until liquid is absorbed. Remove from heat. Leave pan covered to retain heat.

Meanwhile, in a small bowl, whisk together fruit spread, hoisin sauce, vinegar, and red pepper flakes. Set aside.

Heat a 12-inch nonstick skillet over medium-high heat. Remove from heat and lightly spray with vegetable oil spray (being careful not to spray near a gas flame). Cook chicken for 2 minutes, or until just barely pink in center, stirring frequently. (Using two utensils makes handling easier.) Transfer chicken to a plate.

Add oil to skillet. Swirl to coat bottom. Cook onions for 3 minutes, or until beginning to brown, stirring frequently.

Stir in snow peas. Cook for 1 to 2 minutes, or until just tender-crisp, stirring frequently. Stir in salt.

Spoon rice in center of a serving platter. Arrange vegetable mixture around rice.

Return chicken with any accumulated juices to skillet. Add fruit spread mixture. Cook over medium-high heat for 1 minute, or until glazed, stirring constantly. Spoon chicken mixture over rice. Let stand for 3 minutes to absorb flavors.

DIETARY EXCHANGES 1 Starch, 1 Fruit, 1 Vegetable, 3 Very Lean Meat

NUTRIENTS PER SERVING Calories 324; Total Fat 4.5 g; Saturated Fat 0.5 g; Polyunsaturated Fat 1 g; Monounsaturated Fat 1.5 g; Carbohydrates 41 g; Sugar 18 g; Fiber 4 g; Cholesterol 66 mg; Protein 30 g; Sodium 288 mg

Oregano Chicken with Fresh Tomato-Kalamata Sauce

Serves 4; 3 ounces chicken, ¼ cup tomato mixture, and ½ cup barley per serving

- 1¼ cups water
- ⅔ cup uncooked quick-cooking barley
- 1 teaspoon grated lemon zest (optional)
- 5 ounces grape tomatoes or cherry tomatoes, quartered (about 1 cup)
- 12 kalamata olives, coarsely chopped
- ¼ cup snipped fresh parsley
- 1 tablespoon red wine vinegar
- ½ tablespoon olive oil (extra virgin preferred)
- 1 medium garlic clove, minced
- ¼ teaspoon salt
- Vegetable oil spray
- 1 pound chicken breast tenders, all visible fat discarded
- ½ teaspoon dried oregano, crumbled
- ½ teaspoon salt-free lemon-pepper

In a small saucepan, bring water to a boil over high heat. Stir in barley and lemon zest. Reduce heat and simmer, covered, for 10 minutes, or until liquid is absorbed.

Meanwhile, in a medium bowl, stir together tomatoes, olives, parsley, vinegar, oil, garlic, and salt.

Heat a 12-inch nonstick skillet over medium-high heat. Remove from heat and spray with vegetable oil spray (being careful not to spray near a gas flame). Put chicken in skillet. Sprinkle with oregano and lemon-pepper. Cook for 4 minutes, or until no longer pink in center, turning frequently.

To serve, spoon barley onto plates. Arrange chicken on top. Spoon tomato mixture over chicken.

DIETARY EXCHANGES 1 Starch, 1 Vegetable, 3 Very Lean Meat

NUTRIENTS PER SERVING Calories 266; Total Fat 7 g; Saturated Fat 1 g; Polyunsaturated Fat 1 g; Monounsaturated Fat 4 g; Carbohydrates 22 g; Sugar 2 g; Fiber 3 g; Cholesterol 66 mg; Protein 30 g; Sodium 412 mg

Spring Greens with Grilled Chicken and Pineapple-Curry Vinaigrette

Serves 4; 2 cups salad, 2 tablespoons dressing, and
3 ounces chicken per serving

2½ tablespoons sliced almonds
 2 tablespoons flaked sweetened coconut
 1 8-ounce can pineapple tidbits packed in their own juice
 3 tablespoons honey
 2 tablespoons fresh lemon juice
 1 tablespoon cider vinegar
 ½ teaspoon curry powder
 ½ teaspoon grated orange zest
 ¼ teaspoon crushed red pepper flakes
 ⅛ teaspoon salt
 7 cups mixed salad greens (spring mix preferred)
 ¼ cup thinly sliced red onion
 4 boneless, skinless chicken breasts (about 4 ounces each), all visible fat discarded, grilled

Heat a small skillet over medium-high heat. Dry-roast almonds and coconut for 2 minutes, or until coconut begins to turn golden, stirring constantly. Remove from heat. Set aside.

Drain pineapple, reserving ¼ cup juice.

In a small bowl, whisk together ¼ cup pineapple juice, honey, lemon juice, vinegar, curry powder, orange zest, red pepper flakes, and salt.

To assemble, arrange salad greens on a serving platter. Top with chicken breasts. Sprinkle pineapple and onion over salad greens. Pour dressing over all. Sprinkle with almond and coconut mixture.

DIETARY EXCHANGES 1 Fruit, 1 Other Carbohydrate, 3 Lean Meat

NUTRIENTS PER SERVING Calories 253; Total Fat 4.5 g; Saturated Fat 1 g; Polyunsaturated Fat 1 g; Monounsaturated Fat 1.5 g; Carbohydrates 27 g; Sugar 21 g; Fiber 3 g; Cholesterol 66 mg; Protein 29 g; Sodium 178 mg

Cook's Tip

Sweet Salad Dressing: Whenever you want an oil-free sweet salad dressing, you can rely on the thickening power of honey. It gives the dressing the body it needs.

Greek Snapper Fillets with Cucumber-Caper Salsa

Serves 4; 3 ounces fish and ¼ cup salsa per serving

      Vegetable oil spray
  4 **red snapper or tilapia fillets (about 4 ounces each)**
  2 **tablespoons fresh lemon juice**
  ½ **teaspoon dried oregano, crumbled**
  ¼ **teaspoon paprika**
  ⅛ **teaspoon salt**

Cucumber-Caper Salsa

  ¾ **cup finely chopped cucumber**
  ¼ **cup chopped fresh mint or snipped fresh parsley**
  2 **tablespoons capers, rinsed and drained**
  ½ **teaspoon grated lemon zest**
  2 **tablespoons fresh lemon juice**
  1 **tablespoon olive oil (extra virgin preferred)**
  ⅛ **teaspoon salt**

Preheat oven to 400°F. Lightly spray a 13×9×2-inch baking pan with vegetable oil spray.

Rinse fish and pat dry with paper towels. Place fish in a single layer in baking pan. Spoon 2 tablespoons lemon juice over fish. Sprinkle with oregano, paprika, and ⅛ teaspoon salt.

Bake for 10 minutes, or until fish flakes easily when tested with a fork. Using a slotted spatula, transfer fish to a serving platter.

Meanwhile, in a small bowl, stir together salsa ingredients.

To serve, spoon salsa over fish.

DIETARY EXCHANGES 3 Lean Meat

NUTRIENTS PER SERVING Calories 155; Total Fat 5 g; Saturated Fat 1 g; Polyunsaturated Fat 1 g; Monounsaturated Fat 3 g; Carbohydrates 3 g; Sugar 1 g; Fiber 1 g; Cholesterol 42 mg; Protein 24 g; Sodium 339 mg

Sweet Spiced Salmon

Serves 4; 3 ounces fish per serving

- ½ tablespoon grated orange zest
- ¼ cup fresh orange juice
- 2 tablespoons fresh lemon juice
- 4 salmon fillets with skin (about 5 ounces each)
- 1½ tablespoons firmly packed dark brown sugar
- ½ teaspoon paprika
- ½ teaspoon curry powder
- ½ teaspoon salt
- ¼ teaspoon ground cinnamon
- ⅛ teaspoon cayenne
- Vegetable oil spray
- 1 medium lemon, quartered (optional)

Set orange zest aside in a small bowl.

In a large resealable plastic bag, combine orange juice and lemon juice. Rinse salmon and pat dry with paper towels. Add to juice mixture. Seal bag. Turn several times to coat evenly. Refrigerate for 30 minutes, turning occasionally.

Meanwhile, stir brown sugar, paprika, curry powder, salt, cinnamon, and cayenne into orange zest. Set aside.

Preheat oven to 425°F. Line a baking sheet with aluminum foil. Lightly spray foil with vegetable oil spray.

Remove salmon from marinade. Discard marinade. Arrange salmon with skin side down on baking sheet. Rub brown sugar mixture over salmon.

Bake for 14 minutes, or until salmon flakes easily when tested with a fork.

To serve, use a metal spatula to lift salmon flesh from skin. Place salmon on plates. Serve with lemon wedges to squeeze over salmon.

DIETARY EXCHANGES ½ Other Carbohydrates, 4 Very Lean Meat

NUTRIENTS PER SERVING Calories 187; Total Fat 5 g; Saturated Fat 1 g; Polyunsaturated Fat 2 g; Monounsaturated Fat 1.5 g; Carbohydrates 6 g; Sugar 5 g; Fiber 0 g; Cholesterol 74 mg; Protein 28 g; Sodium 388 mg

Cook's Tip

Marinate the salmon for only 30 minutes so the texture will remain firm.

Seaside Shrimp and Sausage Gumbo

Serves 6; 1 cup per serving

1½ tablespoons all-purpose flour
Vegetable oil spray
4 ounces reduced-fat smoked turkey sausage, thinly sliced
3 cups frozen bell pepper stir-fry mix (bell peppers and onions)
1 14.5-ounce can no-salt-added stewed tomatoes, undrained
1¼ cups water
10 ounces frozen sliced okra
1 tablespoon fresh lemon juice (optional)
½ tablespoon sugar
2 medium bay leaves
½ teaspoon dried thyme, crumbled
½ teaspoon red hot-pepper sauce (optional)
¼ cup water
1 cup uncooked rice
8 ounces peeled raw medium shrimp
½ cup snipped fresh parsley
1 tablespoon olive oil (extra virgin preferred)
½ teaspoon salt

Heat a Dutch oven over medium heat. Put flour in Dutch oven and cook for 3 minutes, or until golden, stirring constantly. Pour into a small bowl.

Lightly spray Dutch oven with vegetable oil spray (being careful not to spray near a gas flame). Increase heat to medium-high. Cook sausage for 3 minutes, or until richly browned, stirring constantly. Transfer to a plate and set aside.

Put bell peppers, tomatoes with liquid, 1¼ cups water, okra, lemon juice, sugar, bay leaves, thyme, and hot-pepper sauce in Dutch oven, scraping bottom and sides to dislodge any browned bits.

Whisk remaining ¼ cup water into flour. Stir mixture into gumbo. Bring to a boil over medium-high heat. Reduce heat and simmer, covered, for 30 minutes, or until bell peppers are very soft, stirring occasionally.

Meanwhile, prepare rice using package directions, omitting salt and margarine.

Stir shrimp into gumbo. Cook for 5 minutes, or until shrimp are pink on outside and opaque in center. Remove from heat.

Stir in remaining ingredients, including sausage and rice.

DIETARY EXCHANGES 1½ Starch, 3 Vegetable, 1½ Lean Meat

NUTRIENTS PER SERVING Calories 233; Total Fat 3 g; Saturated Fat 0.5 g; Polyunsaturated Fat 0.5 g; Monounsaturated Fat 2 g; Carbohydrates 38 g; Sugar 7 g; Fiber 3 g; Cholesterol 63 mg; Protein 13 g; Sodium 437 mg

Turkey Breast with Mexican Rub

Serves 8; 3 ounces turkey per serving

Vegetable oil spray

Rub

- **1 teaspoon chili powder**
- **½ teaspoon ground cumin**
- **½ teaspoon dried oregano, crumbled**
- **¼ teaspoon garlic powder**
- **¼ teaspoon black pepper**
- **⅛ teaspoon cayenne**

- **1 3-pound whole turkey breast with skin and bone, gravy packet and all visible fat discarded**

Preheat oven to 325°F. Lightly spray a baking sheet with vegetable oil spray.

In a small bowl, combine rub ingredients.

Pat turkey dry with paper towels so rub will adhere well. Place turkey on baking sheet. Gently separate skin from breast, leaving skin attached at one end. Sprinkle rub over turkey flesh, pressing gently so mixture sticks to flesh. Carefully pull skin over flesh to cover.

Bake for 1 hour 10 minutes, or until turkey is no longer pink in center and internal temperature reaches 170°F. Remove turkey from oven and let stand for 15 minutes. Discard skin before slicing turkey.

DIETARY EXCHANGES 3 Very Lean Meat

NUTRIENTS PER SERVING Calories 132; Total Fat 1 g; Saturated Fat 0.5 g; Polyunsaturated Fat 0.5 g; Monounsaturated Fat 0 g; Carbohydrates 0 g; Sugar 0 g; Fiber 0 g; Cholesterol 80 mg; Protein 28 g; Sodium 56 mg

Broiled Halibut with Herbed Mustard

Serves 4; 3 ounces fish per serving

    Vegetable oil spray
- **4 halibut or other mild fish fillets (about 4 ounces each)**
- **¼ teaspoon salt**
- **¼ teaspoon pepper**
- **3 tablespoons light tub margarine**
- **1 tablespoon Dijon mustard**
- **1 teaspoon grated lemon zest**
- **½ teaspoon dried oregano, crumbled**

Preheat broiler. Line broiler pan with aluminum foil. Lightly spray foil with vegetable oil spray.

Rinse fish and pat dry with paper towels. Place fish on foil. Sprinkle fish with salt and pepper. Lightly spray fish with vegetable oil spray.

Broil fish (on one side only) about 4 inches from heat for 6 minutes (4 to 6 minutes for thinner fish), or until it flakes easily when tested with a fork. Transfer fish to a serving platter. Meanwhile, in a small bowl, stir together remaining ingredients.

To serve, spoon margarine mixture over fish.

DIETARY EXCHANGES 3 Lean Meat

NUTRIENTS PER SERVING Calories 161; Total Fat 6.5 g; Saturated Fat 0.5 g; Polyunsaturated Fat 1.5 g; Monounsaturated Fat 2.5 g; Carbohydrates 1 g; Sugar 0 g; Fiber 0 g; Cholesterol 36 mg; Protein 24 g; Sodium 351 mg

Cook's Tip

Lightly spraying vegetable oil spray on the fish helps keep the fish moist as it cooks.

Stuffed Spinach Rolls

Serves 4; 1 roll per serving

Vegetable oil spray

4 dried whole-wheat lasagna noodles

10 ounces frozen chopped spinach, thawed and squeezed dry

1 cup fat-free or low-fat cottage cheese

1 tablespoon dried basil, crumbled

⅛ teaspoon salt

⅛ teaspoon crushed red pepper flakes

1 cup fat-free, low-sodium spaghetti sauce

½ cup shredded fat-free or part-skim mozzarella cheese

2 tablespoons shredded or grated Parmesan cheese

Preheat oven to 350°F. Lightly spray an 11×7×2-inch baking dish with vegetable oil spray.

Prepare noodles using package directions, omitting salt and oil. Drain well. Blot excess water with paper towels so spinach mixture will adhere to noodles and be easier to handle.

Meanwhile, in a medium bowl, stir together the spinach, cottage cheese, basil, salt, and red pepper flakes.

To assemble, place noodles on a flat surface, such as a cutting board. Spread spinach mixture over each noodle. Starting at one short end, roll up each noodle. Place with seam side down in baking dish, leaving about ½ inch between rolls. Spoon spaghetti sauce over all. Sprinkle with mozzarella.

Bake for 25 minutes, or until thoroughly heated. Remove from oven and sprinkle with Parmesan.

DIETARY EXCHANGES 1½ Starch, 1 Vegetable, 2 Very Lean Meat

NUTRIENTS PER SERVING Calories 203; Total Fat 2 g; Saturated Fat 0.5 g; Polyunsaturated Fat 0 g; Monounsaturated Fat 0 g; Carbohydrates 27 g; Sugar 5 g; Fiber 7 g; Cholesterol 7 mg; Protein 19 g; Sodium 581 mg

Crustless Artichoke and Mushroom Quiche

Serves 5; 2 slices per serving

Vegetable oil spray

1 teaspoon olive oil

8 ounces sliced button mushrooms

1 medium green bell pepper, finely chopped

1 14-ounce can artichoke hearts, rinsed, drained, and coarsely chopped

1½ tablespoons dried oregano, crumbled

⅛ teaspoon cayenne

Egg substitute equivalent to 6 eggs

¼ cup fat-free evaporated milk or fat-free half-and-half

3 medium Italian plum tomatoes (about 2 ounces each), cut crosswise into ⅛-inch slices

⅛ teaspoon salt

¼ cup snipped fresh parsley

1 cup shredded fat-free or low-fat sharp Cheddar cheese

Preheat oven to 350°F. Lightly spray an 11×7×2-inch baking pan with vegetable oil spray.

Heat a large nonstick skillet over medium-high heat. Remove from heat and lightly spray with vegetable oil spray (being careful not to spray near a gas flame). Pour oil into skillet and swirl to coat bottom. Cook mushrooms and bell pepper for 5 minutes, or until bell pepper is tender-crisp, stirring frequently.

To assemble, spoon mushroom mixture evenly into baking pan. Top with artichokes. Sprinkle with oregano and cayenne. Whisk together egg substitute and milk, then pour over all.

Bake for 30 minutes, or until just set in center (doesn't jiggle when gently shaken). Remove from oven.

Arrange tomatoes over quiche. Sprinkle, in order, with salt, parsley, and Cheddar. Let stand for 15 minutes to absorb flavors.

To serve, cut casserole in half lengthwise, then in fifths crosswise. Place 2 pieces on each plate. Serve warm, not hot, for peak flavors.

DIETARY EXCHANGES 3 Vegetable, 2 Very Lean Meat

NUTRIENTS PER SERVING Calories 139; Total Fat 1.5 g; Saturated Fat 0 g; Polyunsaturated Fat 0 g; Monounsaturated Fat 0.5 g; Carbohydrates 14 g; Sugar 6 g; Fiber 3 g; Cholesterol 5 mg; Protein 19 g; Sodium 520 mg

side
dishes

Sesame Broccoli

Serves 4; ½ cup broccoli mixture per serving

- 2 teaspoons sesame seeds
- 2 tablespoons low-salt soy sauce
- 2 tablespoons dry sherry
- 1 tablespoon sugar
- 1 tablespoon cider vinegar
- 1 teaspoon grated peeled gingerroot
- 1 medium garlic clove, minced
- 2 cups broccoli florets (about 10 ounces)

Heat a small skillet over medium-high heat. Dry-roast sesame seeds for 1 to 2 minutes, or until golden, stirring constantly. Pour onto a small plate. Set aside.

Put remaining ingredients except broccoli in skillet. Bring to a boil over medium-high heat. Boil for 1 minute, or until mixture measures ¼ cup. Remove from heat.

Meanwhile, steam broccoli for 4 minutes, or until just tender-crisp.

To serve, put broccoli in a shallow serving bowl. Spoon sauce over broccoli. Sprinkle with sesame seeds.

DIETARY EXCHANGES 1 Vegetable

NUTRIENTS PER SERVING Calories 43; Total Fat 1 g; Saturated Fat 0 g; Polyunsaturated Fat 0.5 g; Monounsaturated Fat 0.5 g; Carbohydrates 6 g; Sugar 4 g; Fiber 1 g; Cholesterol 0 mg; Protein 2 g; Sodium 206 mg

Asparagus with Mild Lemon-Curry Sauce

Serves 4; 5 to 6 asparagus spears and 2 tablespoons sauce per serving

1 **cup water**

1 **pound asparagus, trimmed (20 to 24 thin spears)**

Lemon-Curry Sauce

⅓ **cup fat-free or low-fat plain yogurt**

2 **tablespoons fat-free or light mayonnaise dressing**

2 **teaspoons fresh lemon juice**

¼ **teaspoon curry powder**

¼ **teaspoon salt**

In a large skillet, bring water to a boil over high heat. Add asparagus and return to a boil. Reduce heat and simmer, covered, for 3 minutes, or until just tender-crisp. Drain on paper towels. Place on a serving plate.

Meanwhile, in a small microwave-safe bowl, whisk together sauce ingredients. Cover with plastic wrap. Cook on 100 percent power (high) for 15 seconds. Stir. If sauce is not hot enough, cook, covered, for 10 seconds. Do not bring to a boil (sauce will break down). Pour sauce over asparagus.

DIETARY EXCHANGES 1½ Vegetable

NUTRIENTS PER SERVING Calories 51; Total Fat 0 g; Saturated Fat 0 g; Polyunsaturated Fat 0 g; Monounsaturated Fat 0 g; Carbohydrates 8 g; Sugar 5 g; Fiber 3 g; Cholesterol 0 mg; Protein 4 g; Sodium 224 mg

Yellow Rice with Peppers and Cilantro

Serves 4; ½ cup per serving

- ½ **cup water**
- ½ **cup uncooked quick-cooking brown rice**
- ½ **cup finely chopped onion**
- ½ **medium green bell pepper, finely chopped**
- ¼ **teaspoon ground turmeric**
- 1 **medium tomato**
- 1 **medium fresh jalapeño or ⅛ teaspoon crushed red pepper flakes**
- 2 **tablespoons snipped fresh cilantro**
- 2½ **teaspoons fresh lime juice**
- 1 **tablespoon olive oil (extra virgin preferred)**
- ½ **teaspoon salt**

In a medium saucepan, bring water to a boil over high heat. Stir in rice, onion, bell pepper, and turmeric. Reduce heat and simmer, covered, for 10 minutes, or until water is absorbed. Remove from heat.

Meanwhile, chop tomato. Wearing plastic gloves, cut jalapeño in half lengthwise. Discard seeds and ribs. Finely chop jalapeño.

Stir remaining ingredients, including tomato and jalapeño, into cooked rice mixture.

DIETARY EXCHANGES ½ Starch, 1 Vegetable, ½ Fat

NUTRIENTS PER SERVING Calories 84; Total Fat 3.5 g; Saturated Fat 0.5 g; Polyunsaturated Fat 0.5 g; Monounsaturated Fat 2 g; Carbohydrates 13 g; Sugar 3 g; Fiber 2 g; Cholesterol 0 mg; Protein 2 g; Sodium 297 mg

Acorn Squash with Apricots and Raisins

Serves 4; 1 squash wedge per serving

- **Vegetable oil spray**
- ¼ **cup water**
- 1 **pound acorn squash**
- ¼ **cup raisins**
- ¼ **cup chopped dried apricots**
- 2 **tablespoons firmly packed dark brown sugar**
- ½ **teaspoon ground cinnamon**
- ½ **teaspoon grated orange zest**
- ¼ **cup fresh orange juice**
- ⅛ **teaspoon salt**
- 2 **tablespoons light tub margarine**

Preheat oven to 425°F.

Spray 9-inch baking pan or deep-dish pie pan with vegetable oil spray. Pour the water into pan.

Pierce the skin of the squash with a fork in several places. Cut squash in half vertically. Scoop out and discard seeds and strings. Cut squash in quarters. Place squash, cut side up, in the pan.

In a small bowl, stir together remaining ingredients, except margarine. Spoon onto each squash quarter. Cover pan with aluminum foil.

Bake for 35 minutes, or until squash is tender when pierced with a fork. Transfer squash to plates.

Put margarine in a pan and heat over medium heat until melted. Spoon over squash.

DIETARY EXCHANGES 1 Starch, 1 Fruit, ½ Fat

NUTRIENTS PER SERVING Calories 143; Total Fat 2.5 g; Saturated Fat 0 g; Polyunsaturated Fat 0.5 g; Monounsaturated Fat 1.5 g; Carbohydrates 32 g; Sugar 22 g; Fiber 3 g; Cholesterol 0 mg; Protein 2 g; Sodium 125 mg

Roasted Green Beans and Onions

Serves 4; ½ cup per serving

   Vegetable oil spray
12 **ounces fresh green beans, trimmed**
 1 **medium yellow onion (about 4 ounces), cut into ¼-inch wedges**
 2 **teaspoons olive oil**
 1 **teaspoon Dijon mustard**
 ½ **teaspoon dried tarragon, crumbled**
 ¼ **teaspoon salt**
 ⅛ **teaspoon dried red pepper flakes (optional)**
 2 **tablespoons finely snipped fresh parsley**

Preheat oven to 425°F.

Line a baking sheet with aluminum foil. Lightly spray foil with vegetable oil spray. Place beans (be sure they are very dry) and onion wedges in a single layer on foil. Liberally spray vegetables with vegetable oil spray.

Roast for 10 minutes. Stir. Roast for 8 minutes, or until vegetables begin to brown.

Meanwhile, in a small bowl, stir together the remaining ingredients, except parsley.

To serve, drizzle oil mixture over vegetables. Stir gently to coat. Sprinkle with parsley.

DIETARY EXCHANGES 2 Vegetable, ½ Fat

NUTRIENTS PER SERVING Calories 65; Total Fat 2.5 g; Saturated Fat 0.5 g; Polyunsaturated Fat 0 g; Monounsaturated Fat 1.5 g; Carbohydrates 10 g; Sugar 5 g; Fiber 4 g; Cholesterol 0 mg; Protein 2 g; Sodium 178 mg

Green Peas with Red Bell Pepper Strips

Serves 4; ½ cup per serving

- 2 **cups frozen green peas**
- 2 **tablespoons water**
  Vegetable oil spray
- 6 **medium green onions (white part only), cut into ½-inch pieces**
- ½ **medium red bell pepper, cut into matchstick-size strips**
- ¼ **teaspoon dried oregano, crumbled**
- 1 **tablespoon light tub margarine**
- ¼ **teaspoon salt**

In a medium microwave-safe bowl, combine peas and water. Microwave, covered, on 100 percent (high) for 2 minutes, or until just heated through. Drain well.

Meanwhile, heat a 10-inch nonstick skillet over medium-high heat. Remove from heat and lightly spray with vegetable oil spray (being careful not to spray near a gas flame). Put green onions, bell pepper, and oregano in skillet. Lightly spray vegetables with vegetable oil spray. Cook for 4 minutes, or until vegetables begin to brown on edges, stirring frequently.

Add peas, margarine, and salt. Gently stir until margarine is melted.

DIETARY EXCHANGES 1 Starch

NUTRIENTS PER SERVING Calories 77; Total Fat 1.5 g; Saturated Fat 0 g; Polyunsaturated Fat 0.5 g; Monounsaturated Fat 0.5 g; Carbohydrates 12 g; Sugar 5 g; Fiber 5 g; Cholesterol 0 mg; Protein 4 g; Sodium 253 mg

Fresh Spinach with Zesty Lemon Sauce

Serves 4; ½ cup per serving

Zesty Lemon Sauce

- **2 tablespoons snipped fresh parsley**
- **2 tablespoons light tub margarine**
- **2 teaspoons Dijon mustard**
- **½ teaspoon grated lemon zest**
- **¼ teaspoon salt**

- **⅓ cup water**
- **12 ounces fresh spinach leaves**

In a small bowl, stir together sauce ingredients.

In a Dutch oven, bring water to a boil over high heat. Add spinach. Cook for 1 minute, or until just limp, stirring constantly. (Using two utensils makes handling easier.) Using a slotted spoon, transfer spinach to a shallow serving bowl.

Spoon sauce over spinach, spreading with back of spoon. Let margarine melt before serving.

DIETARY EXCHANGES 1 Vegetable, ½ Fat

NUTRIENTS PER SERVING Calories 43; Total Fat 3 g; Saturated Fat 0 g; Polyunsaturated Fat 0.5 g; Monounsaturated Fat 1.5 g; Carbohydrates 4 g; Sugar 1 g; Fiber 3 g; Cholesterol 0 mg; Protein 3 g; Sodium 310 mg

Roasted Sweet Potato Cubes

Serves 4; about ⅔ cup per serving

    Vegetable oil spray
1 **pound sweet potatoes, peeled and cut into ¾-inch cubes**
2 **teaspoons canola oil**
2 **tablespoons dark brown sugar**
¼ **teaspoon ground cinnamon**
¼ **teaspoon salt**

Preheat oven to 425°F.

Line a baking sheet with aluminum foil. Lightly spray foil with vegetable oil spray. Put sweet potatoes on foil. Drizzle with oil. Toss gently to coat. Arrange in a single layer.

Sprinkle with remaining ingredients.

Bake for 15 minutes. Stir. Bake for 10 minutes, or until very tender when pierced with a fork.

DIETARY EXCHANGES 2 Starch

NUTRIENTS PER SERVING Calories 133; Total Fat 2.5 g; Saturated Fat 0 g; Polyunsaturated Fat 1 g; Monounsaturated Fat 1.5 g; Carbohydrates 27 g; Sugar 11 g; Fiber 3 g; Cholesterol 0 mg; Protein 1 g; Sodium 159 mg

Cook's Tip

For the best texture, be sure to cook the potatoes for the full amount of time recommended.

breads
&
breakfast
dishes

Lemony Sunrise Parfait

Serves 4; ½ cup yogurt mixture, ½ cup fruit, and ¼ cup granola per serving

- 1½ cups fat-free or low-fat plain yogurt
- ⅓ cup confectioners' sugar
- 2 teaspoons grated lemon or orange zest
- 2 tablespoons fresh lemon juice or orange juice
- ¾ teaspoon vanilla extract
- 1 cup fat-free or low-fat granola
- 2 cups blueberries and quartered strawberries

In a medium bowl, whisk together yogurt, confectioners' sugar, lemon zest, lemon juice, and vanilla until confectioners' sugar is completely dissolved.

Spoon 2 tablespoons granola, ¼ cup berries, and about ½ cup yogurt mixture into each wine goblet or parfait glass. Top with remaining 2 tablespoons granola and ¼ cup fruit. Serve immediately.

DIETARY EXCHANGES 1 Starch, 1 Fruit, ½ Skim Milk

NUTRIENTS PER SERVING Calories 189; Total Fat 1 g; Saturated Fat 0 g; Polyunsaturated Fat 0 g; Monounsaturated Fat 0 g; Carbohydrates 40 g; Sugar 25 g; Fiber 4 g; Cholesterol 2 mg; Protein 8 g; Sodium 109 mg

Sweet Corn Muffins

Serves 12; 1 muffin per serving

Vegetable oil spray
1 cup all-purpose flour
1 cup yellow cornmeal
3 tablespoons sugar
1 tablespoon baking powder
¼ teaspoon salt
Dash of cayenne
1 cup fat-free or low-fat buttermilk
Egg substitute equivalent to 1 egg, or 1 large egg
2 tablespoons canola oil

Preheat oven to 425°F. Lightly spray a 12-cup nonstick mini muffin pan with vegetable oil spray.

In a medium bowl, stir together flour, cornmeal, sugar, baking powder, salt, and cayenne.

In a small bowl, whisk together buttermilk, egg, and oil. Add to flour mixture. Stir until just moistened. Do not overmix. Spoon batter into muffin pan.

Bake for 12 minutes, or until a cake tester or wooden toothpick inserted in center comes out clean. Let cool on a cooling rack for 5 minutes before removing from pan.

DIETARY EXCHANGES 1½ Starch, ½ Fat

NUTRIENTS PER SERVING Calories 123; Total Fat 3 g; Saturated Fat 0.5 g; Polyunsaturated Fat 1 g; Monounsaturated Fat 1.5 g; Carbohydrates 22 g; Sugar 4 g; Fiber 1 g; Cholesterol 1 mg; Protein 3 g; Sodium 203 mg

Cook's Tip

It's important to stir the batter only until it is just moistened. Otherwise, the muffins may be tough and will not rise properly.

Sweet Potato Puffy Mini Muffins

Serves 12; 1 muffin per serving

Vegetable oil spray
1 **7.6-ounce package banana muffin mix**
⅔ **cup fat-free milk**
4 **ounces baby food pureed sweet potatoes**
½ **teaspoon ground cinnamon**
½ **teaspoon vanilla, butter, and nut flavoring or vanilla extract**

Preheat oven to 425°F. Lightly spray a 12-cup nonstick mini muffin pan with vegetable oil spray.

In a medium bowl, stir together muffin mix, milk, sweet potatoes, cinnamon, and flavoring until just moistened. Do not overmix. Spoon into muffin pan.

Bake for 15 minutes, or until a cake tester or wooden toothpick inserted in center comes out almost clean. Muffins will continue to cook while cooling. Let cool on a cooling rack for 5 minutes before removing from pan.

DIETARY EXCHANGES 1 Starch

NUTRIENTS PER SERVING Calories 89; Total Fat 2 g; Saturated Fat 0.5 g; Polyunsaturated Fat 0.5 g; Monounsaturated Fat 0.5 g; Carbohydrates 15 g; Sugar 8 g; Fiber 1 g; Cholesterol 0 mg; Protein 2 g; Sodium 109 mg

Oven-Puffed Pancakes (Dutch Baby)

Serves 4; 1 pancake wedge, 2 tablespoons yogurt, and
¼ cup berries per serving

- ½ cup all-purpose flour (see Cook's Tip, opposite)
- ⅔ cup fat-free or low-fat buttermilk
  Egg substitute equivalent to 1 egg, or 1 large egg
  White of 1 large egg
- 2 tablespoons sugar
- 1 teaspoon grated orange zest
- ¼ teaspoon salt
  Vegetable oil spray
- 1 tablespoon corn oil stick margarine, melted
- 2 teaspoons sugar
- ½ cup fat-free or low-fat plain yogurt (optional)
- 1 cup quartered strawberries or 1 cup blueberries

Preheat oven to 425°F.

In a medium bowl, stir together flour, buttermilk, egg substitute, egg white, 2 tablespoons sugar, orange zest, and salt until moistened.

Lightly spray a 9-inch pie pan (regular or deep dish) with vegetable oil spray. Pour in margarine and tilt pan to coat bottom. Pour batter into pan. Do not stir.

Bake for 18 to 20 minutes, or until puffy and golden. The pancake will collapse when removed from the oven.

To serve, sprinkle pancake with 2 teaspoons sugar. Cut into 4 wedges. Place on plates. Top with yogurt and berries. Serve immediately.

DIETARY EXCHANGES 1½ Starch, ½ Fat

NUTRIENTS PER SERVING Calories 156; Total Fat 3.5 g; Saturated Fat 0.5 g; Polyunsaturated Fat 1 g; Monounsaturated Fat 2 g; Carbohydrates 26 g; Sugar 13 g; Fiber 1 g; Cholesterol 2 mg; Protein 6 g; Sodium 267 mg

Cook's Tip

To measure the flour, lightly spoon it into the measuring cup. Level the flour with a knife. This will give you the proper amount—not too much, not packed down, just right—for a successful pancake.

sweet endings

Strawberries with Cinnamon Cream

Serves 4; ½ cup strawberries and 2 tablespoons topping per serving

Cinnamon Cream

- ½ cup frozen fat-free or low-fat whipped topping, thawed
- ¼ cup fat-free or low-fat plain yogurt
- 1 tablespoon firmly packed dark brown sugar
- ¼ teaspoon vanilla extract or ⅛ teaspoon almond extract
- ⅛ teaspoon ground cinnamon

- 2 cups whole strawberries

In a small serving bowl, stir together cinnamon cream ingredients.

Let diners dip strawberries in cinnamon cream, or put strawberries on individual plates or in small bowls and spoon sauce over berries.

DIETARY EXCHANGES ½ Fruit, ½ Other Carbohydrate

NUTRIENTS PER SERVING Calories 59; Total Fat 0.5 g; Saturated Fat 0 g; Polyunsaturated Fat 0 g; Monounsaturated Fat 0 g; Carbohydrates 13 g; Sugar 9 g; Fiber 2 g; Cholesterol 0 mg; Protein 1 g; Sodium 19 mg

Cherry Chocolate Tiramisù

Serves 8; 2×4-inch piece per serving

- 1 **cup water**
- ¼ **cup sugar**
- 2 **teaspoons instant coffee granules**
- 1 **teaspoon vanilla extract**
- 6 **ounces ladyfingers, separated and torn into ½-inch pieces**
- 8 **ounces fat-free or low-fat frozen whipped topping, thawed**
- 2 **tablespoons unsweetened cocoa powder**
- 16 **ounces frozen unsweetened pitted dark cherries, thawed, undrained**
- 2 **tablespoons sugar**
- 1 **tablespoon cornstarch**
- ¼ **teaspoon almond extract**
- ¼ **cup slivered almonds, dry-roasted**

In a small bowl, stir together water, ¼ cup sugar, coffee granules, and vanilla until sugar has dissolved.

To assemble, place ½ of ladyfinger pieces in an 8-inch square baking pan. Stir coffee mixture and spoon half over ladyfingers. Spoon ½ whipped topping over ladyfingers, spreading evenly. Using a fine sieve, sprinkle ½ of cocoa powder over all. Repeat. Cover with plastic wrap. Refrigerate for 8 to 24 hours.

Meanwhile, halve cherries if desired. In a large skillet, stir together cherries and their liquid, 2 tablespoons sugar, and cornstarch until cornstarch is completely dissolved. Bring to a boil over medium-high heat. Boil for 1 minute, stirring constantly. (A flat spatula works well for this so you can scrape bottom, where mixture thickens first.) Remove from heat.

Put skillet on a cooling rack. Stir in almond extract. Let mixture cool completely, about 15 minutes. Refrigerate in a plastic resealable bag or airtight container until serving time.

To serve, spoon cherry mixture over individual servings of tiramisù. Sprinkle with almonds.

DIETARY EXCHANGES 1 Fruit, 2½ Other Carbohydrate, ½ Fat

NUTRIENTS PER SERVING Calories 246; Total Fat 2.5 g; Saturated Fat 0 g; Polyunsaturated Fat 0.5 g; Monounsaturated Fat 1 g; Carbohydrates 51 g; Sugar 32 g; Fiber 2 g; Cholesterol 4 mg; Protein 3 g; Sodium 69 mg

Tropical Mango Cake

Serves 18; 2 × 3-inch piece per serving

    Vegetable oil spray

Cake

  1 18.25-ounce box yellow cake mix with pudding (choose one that calls for 1¼ cups water)

1¼ cups water

  6 ounces baby food pureed pears

    Whites of 3 large eggs

  1 tablespoon grated orange zest

Sauce

  1 cup fresh orange juice

  1 teaspoon cornstarch

  1 tablespoon grated peeled gingerroot

---

  3 medium mangoes, diced

  1 12-ounce container frozen fat-free or low-fat whipped topping, thawed (optional)

  ⅓ cup sweetened flaked coconut (optional)

Preheat oven to 350°F. Lightly spray a 13×9×2-inch baking pan with vegetable oil spray.

In a large bowl, stir together cake ingredients. Using an electric mixer, mix on low speed for 30 seconds, or until moistened. Increase speed to medium and beat for 2 minutes, scraping side occasionally. Pour into baking pan.

Bake for 32 minutes, or until a cake tester or wooden toothpick inserted in center comes out clean. Let cool on a cooling rack for 15 minutes.

Meanwhile, put orange juice and cornstarch in a small saucepan. Stir until cornstarch is completely dissolved. Bring to a boil over medium-high heat. Boil for 1 minute, stirring constantly. Remove from heat.

Stir gingerroot into sauce. Let cool slightly, about 15 minutes.

Using a fork or a cake tester, gently poke holes evenly over cake. Top cake with mangoes. Pour sauce over all. Let cool completely, about 1 hour.

Spread whipped topping over mangoes. Sprinkle with coconut.

With Optional Ingredients:

DIETARY EXCHANGES ½ Fruit, 2 Other Carbohydrate, ½ Fat

NUTRIENTS PER SERVING Calories 196; Total Fat 3 g; Saturated Fat 1.5 g; Polyunsaturated Fat 0 g; Monounsaturated Fat 0 g; Carbohydrates 39 g; Sugar 23 g; Fiber 2 g; Cholesterol 0 mg; Protein 2 g; Sodium 205 mg

Without Optional Ingredients:

DIETARY EXCHANGES ½ Fruit, 2 Other Carbohydrate, ½ Fat

NUTRIENTS PER SERVING Calories 158; Total Fat 3 g; Saturated Fat 1 g; Polyunsaturated Fat 0 g; Monounsaturated Fat 0 g; Carbohydrates 32 g; Sugar 20 g; Fiber 2 g; Cholesterol 0 mg; Protein 2 g; Sodium 191 mg

Very Berry Almond Trifle

Serves 24; ½ cup per serving

- ½ cup sliced almonds
- 16 ounces frozen unsweetened blueberries
- 12 ounces frozen unsweetened raspberries
- ½ cup sugar
- ¼ cup water
- 2½ tablespoons cornstarch
- ¼ teaspoon almond extract
- 2 cups fat-free or low-fat plain yogurt
- 1 teaspoon vanilla extract
- ⅓ cup confectioners' sugar
- 1 1.4-ounce box fat-free, sugar-free vanilla instant pudding (4-serving size)
- 8 ounces fat-free or low-fat frozen whipped topping, thawed
- 1 9-inch angel food cake, torn in small pieces

Heat a large skillet over medium-high heat. Dry-roast almonds for 3 minutes, or until golden, stirring frequently. Transfer almonds to a bowl. Set aside.

In same skillet, stir together blueberries, raspberries, sugar, water, and cornstarch until cornstarch is completely dissolved. Bring to a boil over medium-high heat. Once boiling, remove berries with a slotted spoon and set aside. Reduce heat to medium. Cook for 1 minute to thicken, stirring constantly. Remove from heat and combine with reserved berries.

Stir in almond extract. Let cool completely, about 30 minutes.

In a large bowl, whisk together the yogurt and vanilla. Add confectioners' sugar and pudding mix, whisking until smooth. Fold in whipped topping.

To assemble, in a trifle dish or large bowl, layer ⅓ cake, ⅓ yogurt mixture, and ⅓ berry mixture. Repeat layers. Top with remaining cake

and yogurt. Put remaining berry mixture in an airtight container and refrigerate until needed. Cover trifle dish with plastic wrap and refrigerate for at least 8 hours, or up to 24 hours.

To serve, top trifle with remaining berry mixture. Sprinkle with almonds.

DIETARY EXCHANGES ½ Fruit, 1 Other Carbohydrate, ½ Fat

NUTRIENTS PER SERVING Calories 124; Total Fat 1.5 g; Saturated Fat 0 g; Polyunsaturated Fat 0.5 g; Monounsaturated Fat 0.5 g; Carbohydrates 26 g; Sugar 19 g; Fiber 2 g; Cholesterol 0 mg; Protein 3 g; Sodium 150 mg

Go Red American Heart Association® for women

congratulations!

By buying this book, you are joining the millions of people—women *and* men—who are "going red" to spread the word about women and heart disease and stroke.

The American Heart Association is committed to helping women take charge of their heart health. Our campaign, Go Red For Women, is sponsored by Pfizer and Macy's. It was developed as a national call to women to become more aware of their risk for heart disease and stroke and to learn what they can do to reduce that risk. We do this on behalf of women

Knowledge is power.

Power gives you personal control.

Control leads to a longer, healthier life, so learn the risks and take charge of your health.

Seize this opportunity to protect yourself from heart disease.

everywhere and those who love them.

In today's busy world, many women just don't take the time to take care of themselves. Are you one of them? Only you can do what it takes to learn and live.

Heart disease and stroke are the No. 1 and No. 3 killers of women over the age of 25. Each year cardiovascular diseases claim the lives of about a half-million women. That's more lives than are claimed by the next five causes of death, including breast cancer, combined.

These statistics on women and heart disease may come as a surprise to you. The good news is that you can do a lot to protect yourself when you take the steps needed to recognize and reduce your risks.

The color red evokes passion and confidence—and it signals change. You have the power to help keep your heart healthy. Here's what you can do, starting right now:

- ♥ Learn the warning signs of heart attack and stroke.
- ♥ Schedule regular checkups with your healthcare professional.
- ♥ Keep track of your blood pressure, cholesterol, and weight.
- ♥ Follow your healthcare professional's recommendations, including taking medications as prescribed.
- ♥ Don't smoke. If you do smoke, stop.
- ♥ Eat a balanced diet that is low in saturated fats, trans fats, and sodium.
- ♥ Be physically active.

Call 1-888-MY-HEART (1-888-694-3278) to receive free educational information and the American Heart Association's red dress pin. Visit americanheart.org and click on "Go Red For Women" to sign up for free heart-health programs and to find out how to purchase products that benefit the cause.

Macy's and Pfizer are proud national sponsors of the
American Heart Association's Go Red For Women campaign.

Go Red For Women is brought to you in part by educational grants from
Bayer Aspirin and the PacifiCare Foundation.

it's
not just
a man's
disease

One in five women in the United States has some form of cardiovascular disease.

Cardiovascular diseases are pervasive—and so are the myths about them. One enduring half-truth is that "heart disease is a man's disease." In fact, cardiovascular disease claims the lives of more women than men, and the gap between the number of deaths continues to widen.

Women face six major risk factors for heart disease that often can be prevented, controlled, or treated:

- High blood pressure
- High blood cholesterol
- Tobacco smoke
- Physical inactivity
- Obesity or overweight
- Diabetes

Understanding these risk factors and undergoing early heart-health screening—for both women and men—can help you fight heart disease before it develops.

High Blood Pressure: **The Silent Killer**

High blood pressure, or hypertension, is often called "the silent killer" because it has no obvious symptoms. Your heart and arteries have to work harder when your blood pressure is high, increasing your risk for heart attack and stroke.

Have your blood pressure checked on at least two occasions. If it is high, work with your healthcare professional to make a plan to lower it. The chart below shows ranges of blood pressure (BP) levels, measured in millimeters of mercury (mm Hg), for adults 18 years and older.

Category	SYSTOLIC BP (mm Hg)		DIASTOLIC BP (mm Hg)
Normal	less than 120	and	less than 80
Pre-hypertension	120 to 139	or	80 to 89
Hypertension	140 or higher	or	90 or higher

High Blood Cholesterol: **Risky Numbers**

Cholesterol is a fat-like substance produced by your liver. If your body produces too much, or if you take in extra cholesterol from dietary sources, it can build up with other substances on the inner wall of your arteries. That buildup, called plaque, can narrow the blood vessels and make it harder for your heart to circulate blood. Plaque can rupture and cause blood clots. If a clot blocks a blood vessel to the heart, it causes a heart attack; if it blocks a vessel to the brain, it causes a stroke.

Your healthcare professional can order a lipid profile that measures the levels of cholesterol and other lipids in your blood. If your doctor finds areas of concern, work with him or her to create a diet low in saturated fat and cholesterol, an exercise plan, and a medication regimen if necessary.

As the chart below shows, you're at higher risk if your cholesterol level is 200 milligrams per deciliter of blood (mg/dL) or above.

Category	TOTAL CHOLESTEROL *(mg/dL)*
Desirable: lower risk	Less than 200
Borderline high: higher risk	200 to 239
High: more than twice the risk of desirable level	240 or higher

Tobacco Smoke: No Ifs, Ands, or Butts

Tobacco kills. In fact, smoking is the single most preventable cause of death in the United States. Women who smoke are more likely to die from heart disease or stroke. The solution may not be easy, but it is a choice you can make: If you smoke, quit. If you don't smoke, don't start.

Constant exposure to other people's tobacco smoke at work or at home also increases your risk—even if you don't smoke yourself. Clean indoor air is an important part of your heart health.

Physical Inactivity: Start Moving

You probably already know how good it feels to be active—but you may not realize that consistent inactivity actually increases your risk for heart disease and stroke. The good news is that about 30 minutes of physical activity on most days of the week can help reduce your risk of heart disease. It helps prevent or control high blood pressure, high blood cholesterol, obesity, and diabetes.

Obesity and Overweight: **Lighten Your Risks**

If you carry too much body fat—especially at your waist—your risk increases for high blood pressure, high blood cholesterol, and diabetes. Even if you have no other risk factors, excess weight increases your risk of heart disease and stroke.

Body mass index (BMI) assesses body weight relative to height. To find your BMI, weigh and measure yourself wearing little clothing and no shoes. Multiply your weight in pounds by 703. Divide the product by your height in inches; divide again by your height in inches.

Category	BMI
Underweight	less than 18.5
Healthy	18.5 to 24.9
Overweight	25.0 to 29.9
Obese	30 or higher

With your doctor, decide whether your weight is at a healthy level and how to best manage it.

Diabetes: **Control It for Life**

Most of the food we eat turns into glucose, or sugar, for our bodies to use for energy. The hormone insulin helps glucose enter the cells of the body. When you have diabetes, your body either doesn't make enough insulin or can't use its own insulin as well as it should, or both. This results in increased blood levels of glucose.

Talk with your healthcare professional. A simple blood test can help determine whether your glucose levels are high.

Warning Signs of Heart Attack

- Chest discomfort. Most heart attacks involve discomfort in the center of the chest that lasts more than a few minutes, or that goes away and comes back. It can feel like uncomfortable pressure, squeezing, fullness, or pain.
- Discomfort in other areas of the upper body. Symptoms can include pain or discomfort in one or both arms, the back, neck, jaw, or stomach.
- Shortness of breath. This feeling often comes along with chest discomfort. However, it can occur before the chest discomfort.
- Other signs: These may include breaking out in a cold sweat, nausea, or lightheadedness.

Heart attack and stroke are medical emergencies.

Call 9-1-1. Get to the hospital right away.

Warning Signs of Stroke

- Sudden numbness or weakness of the face, arm, or leg, especially on one side of the body.
- Sudden confusion, trouble speaking or understanding.
- Sudden trouble seeing in one or both eyes.
- Sudden trouble walking, dizziness, loss of balance or coordination.
- Sudden, severe headache with no known cause.

Not all of these warning signs occur with every heart attack or stroke. If you have one or more of these signs, don't wait longer than 5 minutes before calling 9-1-1 for help.

Questions Every Woman Should Ask Her Healthcare Provider

1. What are my risk factors for heart disease?

2. Am I at risk for stroke?

3. What should I know about the effects of menopause on my health?

4. Do I need to lose weight for my health?

5. What is a healthful eating plan for me?

6. What kind of physical activity is right for me?

7. What is my blood pressure? Is that healthy for someone my age?

8. What are my blood cholesterol levels? Are those healthy levels for someone my age?

9. What is my blood glucose level? Is that a healthy level for someone my age?

10. Based on my history and risk factors, what can I do to lower my risk of heart disease and stroke?

Less than half of all women (40 percent) consider themselves well informed or very well informed about heart disease.

how can I go
red?

The American Heart Association offers free programs for women who want to improve their heart health and reduce their risk for cardiovascular disease. You have the power—sign up today and start to take care of your heart.

Choose To Move

Join women of all fitness levels across America who are learning practical ways to increase physical activity. This free 12-week program shows you how to love your body by exercising regularly, selecting nutritious foods, and taking time for yourself. Becoming more active and eating well will help you better juggle work, family, and life's other demands. You'll receive:

- ♥ A personal, easy-to-follow handbook to increase physical activity.
- ♥ Nutrition tips and healthful recipes.
- ♥ Tips on healthy ways to manage your weight and information through online newsletters.
- ♥ Key facts on cardiovascular disease.

Visit americanheart.org or call 1-888-MY-HEART (1-888-694-3278) for more information.

The Go Red For Women campaign is made possible by national sponsorship of Pfizer and Macy's and educational grants from PacifiCare Foundation and Bayer Aspirin.

The Cholesterol Low Down™

This program also helps women—and men—improve their heart health. It offers information about high cholesterol and heart disease, as well as ongoing encouragement and support to help you reach your goals. You'll receive:

- ♥ A brochure that covers many cholesterol-related questions and concerns.
- ♥ A biannual newsletter with cholesterol information and inspiring personal stories.
- ♥ An online global risk assessment to help determine risk for heart disease based on personal risk factors.
- ♥ A cookbook that offers a wide range of delicious recipes.
- ♥ The American Heart Association's *To Your Health*, a practical guide to heart health.

Visit americanheart.org or call 1-800-AHA-USA1 (1-800-242-8721) for more information.

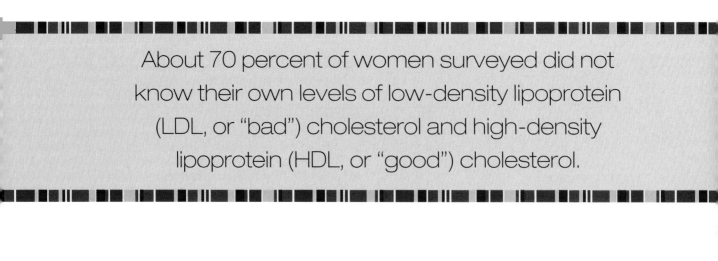

About 70 percent of women surveyed did not know their own levels of low-density lipoprotein (LDL, or "bad") cholesterol and high-density lipoprotein (HDL, or "good") cholesterol.

American Heart Association Food Certification Program

The American Heart Association Food Certification Program is an easy, reliable tool for grocery shoppers. The heart-check mark on food packages indicates that the product meets the American Heart Association food criteria for saturated fat and cholesterol. These criteria apply to healthy people over age two. Heart-check products also meet the Federal Drug Administration criteria that allow food manufacturers to say on the package that the food may help reduce one's risk for heart disease.

For a list of certified products, visit heartcheckmark.org. You can also use our online "Grocery List Builder" to create, print, and take your heart-healthy shopping list to the store.

So look for the heart-check mark when you're shopping.

♥ It's simple.

♥ It's reliable.

♥ It's for you!

get
involved

The American Heart Association brings the latest medical advances into people's lives in many ways. We provide training and science information to medical professionals. We're also actively working to improve emergency care across the country. Our nationwide education programs help people live healthier, more productive lives. These are just a few of the ways we're fighting cardiovascular disease and stroke. We invite you to join us in that fight.

The programs on the next page are examples of how you can make a difference. Please call 1-800-AHA-USA1 (1-800-242-8721) or visit americanheart.org for more information.

Heart Walk: As the signature fund-raising event for the American Heart Association, the Heart Walk promotes physical activity and

heart-healthy living in a fun family environment. Each year more than 750,000 walkers participate in more than 600 events across the country, raising funds to save lives from heart disease and stroke. Join your employer or family and friends in a Heart Walk near you.

Jump Rope For Heart and Hoops For Heart: For the past 25 years, the American Heart Association has made a priority of physical education and teaching the benefits of living a heart-healthy lifestyle to school children. In association with American Alliance for Health, Physical Education, Recreation, and Dance (AAHPERD), these programs teach physical skills while raising funds for heart disease and stroke research.

Train To End Stroke: Completing a marathon is a life-changing event. So is a stroke. The American Stroke Association, a division of the American Heart Association, sponsors this team marathon-training program to raise funds for stroke research and educational programs. Held twice a year, this five-month program provides experienced coaching on how to run or walk a full or half marathon,

along with nutrition information and training clinics. At the end of the training, after reaching their fund-raising goal, teammates run or walk in a marathon held in fabulous locations such as Hawaii, Jamaica, and Florida. For more information on this program and other stroke-related concerns, visit strokeassociation.org or call 1-888-4-STROKE (1-888-478-7653).

tales from the heart
Mary Jane Butac

As an intensive care nurse, Mary Jane Butac of Tacoma, Washington, knew all the warning signs for heart disease—in fact, she had a few of them herself. But she chose to do nothing, preferring to live in denial that anything would happen to her.

However, Mary Jane's carefully constructed excuses began to come apart. In June 2000, the 39-year-old ran in a local race. "I became very short of breath," she recalls. "I thought it was my asthma, so I slowed down and finished the race walking. I didn't give it another thought."

In September, while taking a step aerobics class, Mary Jane again suffered shortness of breath, but this time there was also pain. Not the typical crushing chest pain associated with heart attack, but burning in the left jaw and pain in the left back.

"I was fairly alarmed this time," she says, "and I asked myself what my risk factors were. I knew I had high blood pressure—my average then was 160/90. In addition, I had elevated blood cholesterol, 345. I also had a family history of heart disease with my dad dying at 69 of a heart attack. Last but by no means least, I was obese."

Mary Jane Butac

A trained medical professional, Mary Jane knew that running was giving her a false sense of security. "I thought I was protecting myself by exercising, even though I was not complying with other aspects of a healthy lifestyle," she admits. "Instead, I would run and eat, then run and eat again. But I ate all the wrong things, which kept the weight on and contributed to heart disease."

Mary Jane still did nothing until November, 6 months after her first symptoms—and even then, she approached it indirectly. "At work, I talked to a friend, a cardiac doctor," she says. "I asked in a roundabout way about chest pain. He looked straight at me and asked if I was the one with chest pain. I finally admitted that it was me."

In short order, Mary Jane ended up in the cardiac catheter lab; the next day she had open-heart surgery. Her surgeon found three major vessels that were greater than 70% blocked. She was released a week later and began cardiac rehabilitation.

Mary Jane is running again and is 20 pounds lighter now. She also runs more often than previously, opting for an indoor treadmill when weather restricts outdoor activities. She credits cardiac rehab with turning her life around— indeed, with saving her life. Her blood fats, blood sugar, and blood pressure are now under control with a combination of medications, diet, and exercise.

Learn CPR

The timely use of cardiopulmonary resuscitation (CPR) techniques and automated external defibrillators (AEDs) helps save thousands of lives each year. Learn how to perform CPR in an American Heart Association class, and be ready to save a life. Visit americanheart.org or call 1-877-AHA-4CPR to find a class in your community.

With hindsight, she admits that she was in "denial, denial, denial. I was totally wrong to think I was too young to have this! I needed to make changes if I wanted to live."

Mary Jane is committed to some form of activity daily. "My goal is to do something every day. Running is not my favorite exercise, but it's a confirmation that I have survived heart disease. My biggest goal is to educate women about heart disease."

To accomplish that goal, Mary Jane left intensive care nursing and now specializes in cardiac care. The job switch also allows her more time to shop and cook wisely, for herself and for her husband and son. She is also caring for her mother, who recently suffered a stroke.

"My journey," says Mary Jane, "has been the same journey as that of my cardiac patients. I know what they are going through. I can help them understand that there are things we can do to manage or prevent heart disease or stroke."

tales from the heart
Myra Weinbaum

It may sound funny," says Myra Weinbaum, "but a walk to the mailbox and a little red dress sticker saved my life."

Myra—a 58-year-old part-time school counselor and homemaker from Newington, Connecticut—received in the mail in early February an information packet from the American Heart Association's Go Red For Women awareness campaign. Included in the packet was a red dress sticker to promote awareness of heart attack and stroke.

Myra Weinbaum

"I read the packet and learned that heart disease is the leading cause of death in women, and that women tend to ignore the warning signs," Myra says. She planned to wear the red dress sticker on Friday, February 6, National Wear Red Day For Women.

Like so many other women, Myra had ignored symptoms too. "I'd had a few incidents of rapid heartbeat, but didn't pay any attention to it," she says. "I just waited for it to go away. Besides, I was too young to have a heart problem."

The day after receiving her Go Red For Women information packet, Myra was in the supermarket shopping with her husband, Kenneth, when she felt a rapid heartbeat. Remembering what the packet said about ignoring symptoms, she checked her blood pressure at the in-store machine. It was an alarming 163/120.

The Weinbaums finished shopping and walked out to the car to load groceries. Still thinking about the Go Red packet, Myra suggested to her husband that they stop by the walk-in medical clinic on the way home. "I had it on my mind that women ignore their symptoms," she says. "I wanted a human to check my blood pressure and pulse. I wasn't convinced that the machine was accurate."

The clinic confirmed that Myra's blood pressure was indeed dangerously high, as was her heart rate: 180 beats per minute. An electrocardiogram also revealed abnormal heart rhythms.

"I was the most exciting patient they'd had all day," Myra recalls with a chuckle. "They all came in the room to tell me the readings. Everyone was pretty alarmed."

Clinic staff—concerned that she could suffer a stroke at any moment—ordered an ambulance to transport her to the hospital. At the hospital, Myra was told that she had narrowly averted a stroke as a result of atrial fibrillation, or rapid heartbeat. When the heart beats normally at 75 to 85 times a minute, blood is pumped efficiently through the heart's chambers; when the beat is too fast, blood is not pumped efficiently, causing it to pool and form clots. The clots then circulate in the blood, resulting in stroke.

Myra spent three days in the hospital while her health, medications, and lifestyle were evaluated. She was released in time to be home for her birthday.

The lesson learned? "I wasn't too young to have heart-related health issues," Myra says. "I now realize how fortunate I was to catch my stroke before it happened. Now, instead of ignoring symptoms, I'm on the lookout for anything suspicious. And if it hadn't been for the Go Red For Women packet I received in the mail the day before, I wouldn't have gone to the walk-in clinic. I would have just stayed at home, ignoring my symptoms.

"I can't stress it enough. Take warning signs seriously. Don't think it's nothing. It's better to be safe than sorry. I'm living proof of that."

Learn and Live Quiz

For a personal assessment of your risk factors for heart disease and stroke, take the free Learn and Live quiz. It's quick and easy—and it could be your first step toward better health. Visit americanheart.org for an online quiz, or call 800-AHA-USA1 (800-242-8721), and we'll send you a free copy of the quiz to take at home.

tales from the heart
Renee Kowalski

Renee Kowalski is the first to admit that she's a fortunate person. A homemaker in Sunnyvale, Texas, she enjoys a successful husband, two great kids, a passion for tennis, and glowing health.

Life, however, has a way of throwing curves. Three years ago, while playing tennis, Renee, then 48, felt a weight on her chest. Her first thought? Perhaps it was a cramp or her bra strap was too tight. She continued playing, and the sensation of pressure went away.

"I played tennis over the next several months," she recalls, "but my friends started telling me that I wasn't getting to the ball. This was odd—I was always a jackrabbit."

About that time, Renee's husband, Michael—deciding to get into shape—purchased a five-year contract at a fitness center. "It was the rainy season," says Renee, "so I thought I would go too.

Renee Kowalski

"The machines had warning labels saying to check with a physician before beginning any exercise program. I was adamant about my husband getting checked, and he was fine." However, Renee didn't get herself checked out.

Once on the treadmill, she again found herself experiencing chest pain—and this time it scared her. "When we got home, I was concerned. The pain didn't go away as quickly as it had before. My husband called the doctor."

During an electrocardiogram/treadmill test, Renee did fine walking, but chest pains returned when the pace was pumped up. "The test was stopped," she says, "and I had to go lie down." She had an 80% blockage in one artery and some blockage in two others; a day later she had triple bypass surgery.

Renee's friends and tennis partners were stunned. "No one thought it could be me," she says. "I had a low-stress life as a stay-at-home mom, played competitive tennis regularly, and had normal cholesterol, blood pressure, and weight. My friends all had their hearts checked!"

Today Renee's life is better than ever, with one important change: the food she prepares. "My body clogs its arteries even though I have low cholesterol, so I decided to cook healthier, just to be on the safe side. I used to make banana bread, for example, with the eggs, butter, and sugar. Now I make it with heart-healthy oils, egg whites, and applesauce to reduce fats and sugar. I can still eat foods that taste really good, but they're good for my heart as well."

In a recent survey by the American Heart Association, only 13 percent of women said they consider heart disease their greatest health risk.

Renee learned about healthier foods and cooking techniques from an American Heart Association cookbook a friend gave her after surgery. "The AHA cookbooks taught me how to be more aware when it comes to health, and how to eat healthier." Now she makes over her family's favorite recipes using techniques from the AHA cookbooks.

Renee had other adjustments to make, too—including dealing with survivor guilt and pushing herself physically again. "Why did I get the warning signs? Why did I survive? The doctor told me if I had had a heart attack, I would have died." She got through with her faith and the knowledge she gained in rehab. "Rehab taught me not to be afraid," Renee says. "I understand now that I can still have quality of life, and an active life. In fact, I have more energy now than ever. I can do a quicker mile and I have no concerns about getting my heart pumping.

"I want people to know when they do get those warning signs, don't be in denial like I was. I'm still here because I did get checked out and didn't have a heart attack."

tales from the heart
Valerie Greene

Valerie Greene was a young woman going places. At 31, she was a successful businesswoman, the owner of a thriving estate financial planning firm in Winter Park, Florida. With an athletic figure, perfect health, and a thousand-watt smile, the outgoing Valerie had everything to live for.

One night after work in 1996, however, a headache changed everything. "I didn't think much of it and went to lie down," Valerie recalls. Six months later, she became extremely dizzy and disoriented. She went to the doctor, but nothing definitive was diagnosed. Perhaps it was vertigo, she was

Valerie Greene

told. Ten days after that, Valerie's speech became slurred and one side of her body became numb, and she again went to the hospital.

"I was told to go home to 'sleep it off!'" says an indignant Valerie. "They thought I was drunk, because I was too young to have a stroke. Then they said I might have multiple sclerosis. I refused to leave, and 36 hours later I stroked in the hospital."

Misdiagnosing stroke is not uncommon, especially in women and younger people. In Valerie's case, a blood vessel to her brain was blocked by a large blood clot, allowing no oxygen to reach that part of the brain. "I woke up in ICU, paralyzed on my entire left side, with hearing loss in my right ear and unable to speak," she says. "I was kicking and screaming on the inside but unable to move or articulate my feelings on the outside. It was a horrifying and frightening living hell."

Valerie was told she might never walk again; she was hospitalized for four weeks while undergoing close monitoring and extensive rehabilitation. Completely helpless, she had to learn how to crawl again; she admits that she became depressed and even thought about suicide. She was released into the care of a full-time home health nurse—but only after she demonstrated she could say a single word: "Help." She left the hospital in a wheelchair.

Today, nearly eight years after her strokes, Valerie is a public speaker on behalf of stroke awareness. She has written a book, "The Fire Within: A True Story of Triumph Over Tragedy" (Alex Press 2004). She's a half-marathon athlete, walking 13.1 miles, and was the nation's top fund-raiser for the American Stroke Association's Train To End Stroke program in 2003. She also lobbied on behalf of the Florida Stroke Act, which ensures that any suspected stroke victim is transported to a qualified hospital with special triage training and protocols to recognize stroke.

Valerie can no longer perform the complex financial calculations she used to do with ease. She still deals with some speech and physical deficits. However, she has no regrets about the unexpected directions stroke has propelled her life. "I have become a motivational speaker and a writer as a result of stroke," she says. "If I can show how well I have overcome two strokes, perhaps I can encourage other stroke survivors to stay in therapy—recovery comes in the form of small, incremental improvements. Please, don't give up!"

Valerie believes the strokes also helped her find her way in life's spiritual journey. "I had to dig deep and find my fire within and ignite it," she says. "Something pulled me out of the depths of hell, and I survived to tell the story."

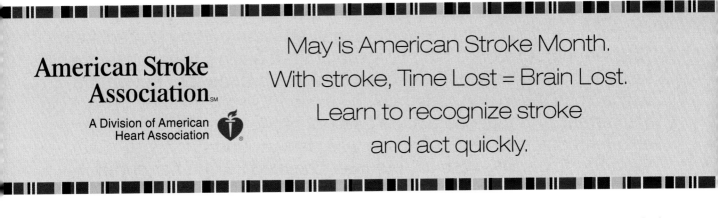

tales from the heart
Evelyn Young

Evelyn Young

Evelyn Young, a busy flight attendant, simply did not have time to be sick. Though the mom and grandmother from Plano, Texas, had felt dizzy after a tennis game the night before, she shrugged it off because the dizziness went away when she stood still.

The next morning Evelyn felt fine and caught a train to the airport—but on the train, something wasn't right. She knew that she was speaking to someone but making no sense.

She checked into the flight office and boarded her plane, but a crew member quickly realized something was wrong. "My speech went crazy, incoherent," Evelyn says. "I asked another attendant what was wrong with me, and she said the only thing she could think of was stroke."

Evelyn, then 64, was not convinced—to her, a stroke meant a physical disability, not a speech problem. She worked the flight with her duties reassigned to minimize passenger contact, but three hours later, on another flight preparing to take off, she wasn't any better.

"Something told me to get off the plane," she says. She was taken by her supervisor to the medical office, where paramedics transported her to the hospital. A CAT scan at the hospital revealed that Evelyn had suffered a stroke, with no apparent underlying cause.

Hospitalized for a month, Evelyn began speech therapy immediately. She returned to work—but soon she started having headaches, then her vision deteriorated. She transferred to a ground job, but on the way across the airport to a training session, Evelyn realized her driving was erratic and that she couldn't see all of the letters in signs. She also felt confused, and her vision was dark around the edges. She went to the training session, but later checked in with her doctor, complaining about her eyes.

"He looked at me and said, 'Ev, this isn't about your eyes. This is a stroke.'"

She was 65 and just a year past her first stroke. A biopsy was performed to look for causes; brain surgery revealed that protein clusters were blocking blood vessels, causing them to break and bleed, resulting in stroke. The condition, cerebral amyloid angiopathy, usually doesn't occur in people younger than 70; Evelyn survived a third stroke two years later, at age 67.

Evelyn didn't seem like a stroke candidate. She didn't smoke or drink, wasn't overweight, didn't eat junk food, and had normal cholesterol and blood pressure. No one knows what causes amyloid angiopathy, and there is no cure. "My doctor told me I just have to live with it, and to go out and live my life," says Evelyn.

She's doing exactly that. Five years after her first stroke, Evelyn can see, speak, and read again, though she does cope with some deficits. "I know exactly what I want to tell you," she says, "but I can't always get it out the way I'm thinking, and my speech slurs a little when I'm tired." None of that stops Evelyn from being a motivational speaker for stroke awareness. "I believe God saved me because I have work to do in the health field. I want people to understand that stroke doesn't just happen to older people—even kids have strokes."

Most of all, she says, women have to learn to take better care of themselves. "I just met a lady who had a stroke," Evelyn says. "She got out the heating pad, thinking that would help, instead of going to the hospital. Like me, a lot of women are in denial."

"I meet so many people with stroke. It really breaks my heart. I want people to know that they can get better if they just believe in themselves, like I did."

index

American Heart Association Consumer Publications

Eat well and take care of your heart with recipes from the American Heart Association's best-selling library of cookbooks. Look for these and other American Heart Association publications wherever books are sold.